ONE BLUE STAR

ONE BLUE STAR

POEMS ABOUT THE MILITARY, FAMILIES, WAR AND PEACE

By

Mindy Phillips Lawrence

Published by Red Engine Press

"Sand", "Media War", "A Soldier's Wife" and "Caissons" first published by *South End Poetry Anthology,* 2004

"Duty Call" first published at www.goodgoshalmighty.com and later appeared in *South End Poetry Anthology,* 2004

"The Handshake" first published at www.poetsagainstthewar.org

The cataloging in publication data is on file with The Library of Congress

ISBN 0 9745652 5 3

Cover design and illustrations by Mindy Phillips Lawrence

Printed in the United States of America

Quantity discounts are available on bulk purchases of this book for educational institutions or social organizations. For information, please contact the publisher:
Red Engine Press
P.O. Box 6255
Key West, FL 33040

MY BLUE STAR DEDICATION

This book is dedicated to my son, Grant B. Lawrence, of the Army's 101st Airborne Division (Air Assault) stationed in Ft. Campbell, KY, and all of our soldiers who have been called to duty. It is also dedicated to his brother, Daniel P. Lawrence, who entered the service but was released for medical reasons. Daniel, spared the trials of fighting in a foreign land, serves his country in a different way – as a firefighter.

Grant completed Army Basic Training and Advanced Individual Training (AIT) in January of 2003 and left for Kuwait in February 2003. He entered Iraq with the invasion force, was briefly stationed in Baghdad then headed north to the city of Mosul. He returned to the United States in February 2004 without physical harm. I can't imagine the conditions he faced or the sights he saw while he was there.

My Blue Star Banner hangs proudly in my front window. May its star never change color!

ACKNOWLEDGEMENTS

Until you assemble a book, you have no idea how much work goes into it. Had I not had the help of the people I did, this project would never have been completed.

My thanks goes to Joyce Faulkner for editing assistance, allowing me to ask many questions and motivating me to continue when I wasn't sure I knew how to say what I wanted to say. I thank her for being my Pondering Partner in Pittsburgh who has never shied away from kicking me when I needed it.

If it weren't for writer and editor Bev Walton Porter, I would never have begun writing again, met the writers I work with now or kept going when I'd lost my energy. I thank her for the help and instruction she has given me to write on a professional level and thank her for her kind foreword.

I thank J.R. Faulkner for the finished book design and set up of *One Blue Star*. Also, were it not for Red Engine Press and its founder, Jim Radzinski, this book would never have been published.

I must also thank my sons, Daniel and Grant for being kind enough to leave me alone when I was writing and for Grant's wife, Jennifer, for making him inaccessible at the right moments. Even when my sons disagreed with what I was saying, they discussed the issues with me as adults and made me very proud to be their mom.

And I can't forget my young friend, Amber Page, the sweet young lady who comes up behind me and gives my neck a rub when I've been at the keyboard too long. She's the closest thing to a daughter I will ever have.

FOREWORD

The Internet can be an impersonal place. Like ships passing in the night, you often meet people, chat with them briefly, and then continue on your journey toward the next informative, yet stimulating, mailing list or Web site. Some people make such an impression, however, that you end up becoming life long friends. What began as a connection borne from e mail messages carried through the ether, seats itself as a real and concrete relationship. This is how I came to know Mindy Phillips Lawrence.

In 2000, Mindy signed up for a freelance writing course I taught online. Through the course I came to know many students. Mindy was a bright ray of sunshine from the beginning. She was eager, determined, and talented. After the course, we maintained contact and got to know each other not only as sister scribes, but as human beings and, eventually, friends. When my husband unexpectedly died in 2001, it was the blackest period of my life. Thanks to close, caring friends like Mindy, I picked up the shattered pieces and believed I could live again. In a twist of fate, she became my teacher and motivator – after nine months of not writing, she held my hand and helped me regain faith in myself. She is an earthbound angel who went from my student to my teacher.

It is through *One Blue Star* that her inimitable light continues to shine. We live in troubled times where the ravages of war scar our psyche and our souls daily. By the artistry of her poetry, Lawrence puts a human face on this war in which we are engaged. She stirs up vivid images that force us to pause and reflect on the battles being waged both on and off the field – battles fought and sealed not only in blood, but in the depths of faith as well. The human condition is delicate and unified. Whether it is a soldier in Afghanistan or a Muslim in Baghdad, we all have our missions. *One Blue Star* urges readers to remember that despite religious or ethnic differences, there is one condition we share – that of being human. Within these pages, Lawrence compels us to reconnect with our commonalities, not only for the sake of our loved ones, but also for the sake of the world's future generations.

Bev Walton Porter
August 2004

ONE BLUE STAR

DUTY CALL

If I walk down the hallway,
The path leading to your room,
The same way you walked when you were here,
I see the remnants of your life,
Ashtray at the ready for your habit,
Bedclothes jostled as if you just left.

I will step over boots and shirts and other things
That speak your name without speaking.
As the light goes on and I hear the fan's slow hum,
I will not expect to see you there,
Although I feel your presence.
You packed your bag   then you were gone.

I held the door for you
And watched you as you walked away
You one direction, I the other.
I didn't have the strength to see you go,
But I have the strength to wait for your return.
Funny how I know you will come home.

I went down the hall this morning.
I rearranged your bed and straightened your clothes.
The ashtrays are empty and cleaned for your next draw.
The fan is off. No use to run it when you cannot hear its song.
I have the door unlocked
In case you come home while I'm sleeping.

~Published at www.goodgoshalmighty.com and in the 2004 *South End Poetry Anthology*

SAND

Sand in a glass,
Shifts down the sides at
Gravity's demand.
The particles pile
Upon one another
Until they are one mass,
Gathered at the bottom.

You and I are particles
Shifted by time.
Dispersed by the orders of
A man with no sons to give.
Since he has none, he takes mine,
Uniting him with all the others
Gathered in the sand.

~Published in the 2004 *South End Poetry Anthology*

WEST OF AFGHANISTAN

Osama, Osama
Won't you come out?
We are looking for you.
We only want to talk –
To get to know you better.

What's that, you say?
You aren't in Baghdad?
We thought you were.
That is where we searched.
We went west. Was that wrong?

They say you're the mastermind
Of the Two Towers. Are you Sauron?
If so, why are we in
Saddam's country fighting?
Should we not be where you are?

We are just west of Afghanistan.
Hopscotching over Iran,
Flip flopping over Persia
To Babylon.
Maybe we will find you there.

MEDIA WAR

There they were,
The media men
Embedded in the fray
Like rocks in sod,
Cameras rolling.

Too close.
A truck turns over.
The reporter pinned
Under his story,
Calls out.

No one hears him
Over the hubbub.
The troops move on,
Missing the man
In trouble.

He lies in the ditch,
Watching his life
Ebb away, reporting
On his own demise
As he can.

He thinks of his home,
His job, his country,
As the heat rises
With the sun
And death.

A passing soldier
Sees the reporter,
Lifeless now,
Who met his
Final deadline.

~Published in the 2004 *South End Poetry Anthology*

A SOLDIER'S WIFE

She sits quietly,
Painting her fingernails bright red.
Her blonde waves
Fall over her shoulders.
Where is he today, she wonders?
The headlines tell all.

She looks at her hand.
There's a wedding ring
With no husband attached.
She remembers a wedding night,
Then loneliness.

She goes to a restaurant
Alone, buying dinner for one.
When she finishes, she washes
The car. A yellow ribbon flows
From her antenna.

She straightens their apartment,
Then turns back the covers
On one side of the bed.
On the other side, the sheets
Never move.

~Published in the 2004 *South End Poetry Anthology*

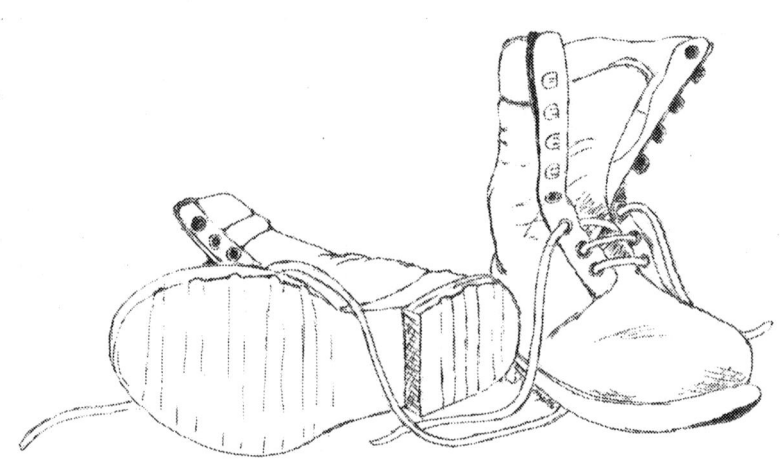

THE HANDSHAKE

Through the battlefield we drove
After all the armies left the theater.
Burning hunks of metal greeted us,
Along with the smell of death.

We passed through.
Unaccustomed to the aftermath,
We stood with shell shocked faces
Looking at the conflagration.

Then we saw the hand,
Nothing else was there, no head or body,
Just five fingers and a wrist
Beside the road.

So we stopped. Each one of us,
Both appalled and amazed,
Bent down and shook the cold fingers;
Made a ceremony of it.

We laughed at its touch,
Made light of its grasp on us
Not physical, but mental.
Although we saw it differently.

It was nothing,
An invisible enemy taken apart
And dropped on the desert floor.
We left it and moved on.

Down the road,
Our laughter ceased.
We fell silent
Thinking of a man without a hand.

~Published at *Poets Against the War* (www.poetsagainstthewar.org)

CAISSONS

You used to play
With Tonka trucks.
Matchbox cars and John Deere tractors rolled
Across the bedroom floor.

But boys grow up
And seek other wheels.
Mustangs and racecars speed down country roads.
Looking for excitement.

Now Humvees and tanks growl
In the desert air,
As you haul one more cannon up a hill
Gaining position.

Life used to be so simple,
Clean the toys from the floor
And put them up for the next race.
Now all I hear is the deafening sound of war.

~Published in the 2004 *South End Poetry Anthology* and *Poets Against the War* (www.poetsagainstthewar.org)

BABYLON IS FALLING

"Babylon the great is fallen, is fallen..."~REVELATIONS 18:2

In the years of Nebuchadnezzar,
Amyitis, daughter of the King of Medes,
Grieved for her homeland.
Betrothed to the lord of Babylon
For convenience, not desire,
She remembered the lush land
Of her youth; the rugged mountains
Reflecting sunlight and carrying the scent
Of trees.

Here was Amyitis in a barren world,
In flat, sun baked Mesopotamia.
Unable to thrive in a place
With no flowers.
She stumbled to a window, sand in her eyes
And saw emptiness.
No brightly colored stones were there
To greet her; no water to plant a garden,
Or tend it.

It was then that Nebuchadnezzar saw
Her tear stained face and heard her sighs.
It pained him to see such beauty suffer
At his hand. How might he ease her sorrows?
How might he bring her nearer to her homeland
And to his heart?
He had built temples, streets and palaces.
What if he constructed a garden
For her pleasure?

He called the royal engineers who conjured figures,
And drafted plans with the king watching.
Soon they developed a miraculous idea.
Bricks were baked to take the place of stones
Long missing from the landscape.
Step by step, the wonder took shape.
Terraces rose like graduated mountains
Resting on cube shaped pillars hollowed out
For trees to grow.

The Euphrates wound near the site,
But its waters were not near enough
To pour their life onto the garden.
Nebuchadnezzar called his mathematicians,
Engineers and soothsayers.
They produced water engines,
Raising the Euphrates into the garden.
Large wheels bore the water higher
In buckets.

All this he did for Amyitis, the queen.
And she, so long saddened by a
Desert land, smiled at the beauty of flowers,
Of color hanging down from walls
Around the city. Of trees where birds could sing,
Of waterfalls and blooms and life.
She thanked Nebuchadnezzar, the king,
For making her feel
At home.

Then did King Nebuchadnezzar die.
Soon the Persians came. The Gardens were
Destroyed, and the land became
Barren again. The ornate walls of Babylon
And their gardens, passed away into
Archaeology.
It was on that spot a soldier stood on a
Warm March morning, driving toward Baghdad,
His weapon on his shoulder.

He did not know the history of the place,
But saw the ruins before him,
He was part of another army come to view
One of the Seven Wonders,
Part of the chain of time marching through
The Cradle.
If the war gods allowed, he would make it home
To learn more about the walls and pillars.
He snapped a photo, freezing the antiquity
In time.

THE RESERVIST

"When the rich make war, it's the poor that die."
~*Jean Paul Sartre*

It seemed a simple choice;
A few weekends for
Money, college, maybe a car.
The chance to make a difference,
To be somebody special,
Be all he could be.

Maybe, down the road,
A way out of a little town
With no possibilities.
The man at the office told him,
He would be rewarded,
His country needed him.

He signed the papers and
Everything changed.
The recruiter's job was done.
The soldier went to training then
Came back home, waiting;
But not for long.

Soon he packed his bags and
Left for a foreign land,
Just for a little while, he thought.
Then he stayed a little longer,
Waiting for replacements.

A year later, he stood at a
Crossroad. He, a mechanic,
Worked on the stalled truck on the
Side of the road. He lowered the hood
As the attack began.

His mother cried at the news.
She welcomed him back,
Propelling his wheelchair at the
Airport with mingled pride and grief.
The soldier was home.

He was home without work,
With few benefits and wounded,
He tried to make sense of it.
He was a weekend warrior come home
To find opportunity gone.

HOLY WAR

Ghazzi bin Abdullah walked near a wall
Pondering the wisdom of Allah.
Trained in the art of combat,
He slipped through the city
Undetected.

He heard the cry from the parapets.
Turning east, he placed his carpet
on the ground. "Allah is good,"
He said, knowing that greatness
Was on his side.

Daniel Morgan James heard the call to prayer.
He thought how misguided men were
Who worshipped a god who demanded attention
Five times a day. He opened his Bible,
Considering a passage.

"Let them be ashamed who seek my soul.
Let them be driven backward and put to shame
That wish me evil," he said.
Surely he would be victorious against those
Who sat on a carpet to pray.

Ghazzi bin Abdullah rolled up his mat.
He shouldered his gun and moved on.
Convinced of his success, he came around
The corner as Daniel Morgan James approached.
Ghazzi bin Abdullah slid behind a gate.

As Daniel Morgan James drew closer,
He saw a shadow. "My God will protect me,"
He said, as he placed his rifle in his hands.
He stepped behind a barrier and waited
For the moment to ripen.

Ghazzi rushed Daniel's position,
The pop of bullets sounded through the streets,
Daniel crouched behind a cold stone wall,
Waiting for an opportunity.
When it came, he was prepared.

Both men fired on one another.
A pain hit Daniel Morgan James
Under his arm. His vest spared him from
Destruction at the optimum moment.
God was surely on his side.

Ghazzi rushed his prey with the words
Of Allah in his mouth. A bullet found him,
Spun him around and prostrated him
In the dust by the American's feet.
"Praise God," Daniel whispered.

The Muslim was mortally wounded.
He would soon be martyred
For his faith. He only had one last gift
To give Allah before he departed.
He raised his gun and shot the American again.

Daniel Morgan James felt the metal enter
His temple. His last thought was, "Why?"
God promised victory, as Allah promised victory.
Both men lay in the street,
Martyrs to their deity.

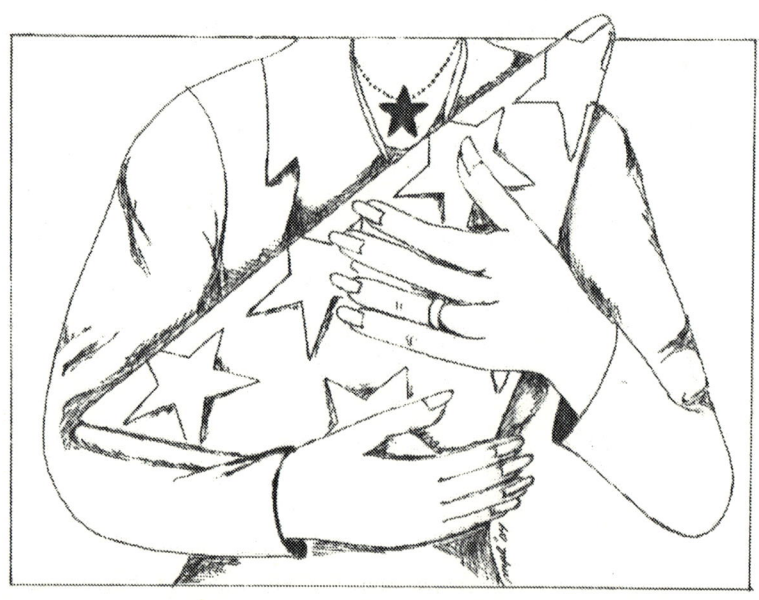

TRIANGLE

On a crisp day in spring,
A young woman sat
In a folding chair with a
Velvet slipcover.
She sat quietly,
Responding with no response,
Her mind on the day the call came,
"We regret to inform you."

A man approached
In full dress uniform, clutching a
Triangle folded with dignity,
Showing a field of blue
With white stars.
He offered it to her
As a substitute for
Her husband.

She would put it
In a display case,
Remembering the day
She received it. The child
Inside her would not recall.
She was a woman,
Representing all women,
Who bury a soldier.

ARIEL

The gazelle pranced through the street.
Stopping at a corner,
He took an inquisitive look,
Unaware of the hunter's gaze.

He stood there,
Alert,
Ears perked up.
Listening to the pulse of the city.

Should he turn left or right?
Which was the path to safety?
His senses made the decision
And he turned near the building.

The hunter struck.
Mortally wounded, the gazelle collapsed
In the confusion of morning.
Precious one, could you not have turned the other way?

Dedicated to the memory of Sgt. Ariel Rico
101st Airborne
Killed in Action   11/03 in Iraq

CASTE

I am an American
I rise before dawn and take
The El to work
I arrive at the plant ready
To pass through another day,
My work orders in hand.
My son serves in the Army.

I am an American.
I live in California and
Carry my children to childcare
Before I start my day.
Trabajo muchas horas para
Cuidar de mi familia.
My son is in the Marines.

I am a woman in Tennessee.
I am an American by choice
After escaping a cruel dictatorship.
I work at a clothing store and
Save pennies, hoping to start
College someday,
My daughter is in the National Guard.

I am an American.
I work in New York City in a high rise
Overlooking the remnants of
What used to be.
I tuck my newspaper under my arm
And go to the office to conduct business.
My son is in the Navy.

Many years ago, my family moved
To this country,
We were poor, as we still are,
But richer now than we have been.
I own a small restaurant in St. Louis
Where I serve ethnic foods.
My son is in the Air Force.

I am the President of the United States.
I am an American.
That's all I have to say.

WHERE I STAND

White, Anglo Saxon Protestant, I
See life through the filter of
Values family taught me
What to believe, what to think,
How to react to different people
I lived near in the South.
Role models matter.

Family taught me about religion,
Leaving me at church as they
Drove home on a Sunday morning.
They taught me about race,
Saying there was no difference,
Then showing difference to me
With their actions.

They taught me about politics,
D.C. was the Devil,
Why would I want to go there?
What good to see the White House,
Congress or the Pentagon?
What good to see statues of men
Who died for our country?

When sheltered people grow up,
They shed the thoughts of family,
One by one, as they read and
Study for themselves instead of
Listening to what others believe.
They begin to understand the sound of
Mendacity.

Some never break free.
Some never pick up a paper,
Read a book, watch a movie,
Listen to newscasts.
They allow others to think for them.
Some never study to make themselves
Approved.

Then the media decides who is president,
The neighbor decides who a friend votes for.
The relative decides how race is handled.
A sect decides gays are evil.
A child is born into the family and again,
The lessons repeated, another generation
Learns not to think for themselves.

DON'T CALL ME NAMES

The parade goes by.
Soldiers in a row set out to fulfill
Their mission.
Commanded to go,
They pack their belongings and
Leave their families
Behind.

I see him
In the rank and file with the other
Sons and daughters.
My brave soldier son going away
To do his duty,
Leaving me
Alone.

I have a question.
Do I love him less
Because I speak out
Against that command?
Do I think less of his comrades
Because I think little
Of their
Orders?

What of my country?
Do I love it less because
I speak up on issues
I believe in?
Doesn't the Constitution
Give me that
Right?

Don't call me names,
Unless you call me an American mother,
An American woman,
An American citizen.
If I don't agree with you,
That is my
Decision.

I think for Myself.
I know men paid
The price for my right
Of dissent.
You have the right to disagree.
I don't call YOU Un American.
For taking another side.

THE CITIZEN'S TASK

"Whenever the people are well informed, they can be trusted with their own government." ~Thomas Jefferson

Who guards the gates to our minds
When we leave them open for
Genius and rubbish to come in?
When citizens refuse to read,
They remain ignorant.
They become pawns,
Gathering thoughts from others
Without learning for themselves.

The liberty of all is interesting to all,
For, when the freedom of one is reduced,
The freedom of all is curtailed.
A country cannot survive without
Knowing for itself.
Our citizens cannot remain great if
Others tell them what to think.

It is our responsibility to stay informed,
Learn the issues, ignore surface battles; to
Dig down into what we need as a country.
Our underlying needs are crucial.
We can listen to the bickering of politicians
Or study what they stand for.
It is our decision whether we remain anesthetized
Or wake up and learn for ourselves.

ENLACES

"America is so beautifully diverse. We are truly Joseph's coat of many colors and tongues and cultures, all blended together into a kind of tapestry."~Joyce Faulkner

We see through different eyes a many colored nation
Viewing heaven and earth from our own perspective.

The constellations are the same for a
White woman in Gettysburg as for a
Black woman in Atlanta.
The Hispanic man in Texas sees the same moon
As the Bosnian man in St. Louis.
The sun shines on the Jew in Denver,
And the Saudi in Los Angeles.
It glows for the Creole in New Orleans,
And the Latvian in Des Moines,
The same planets circle us all.

We speak in the tongues of the world,
All in one country.
America speaks English, Spanish and Portuguese;
Korean, Urdu and Mandarin;
Czech, German and Danish;
Russian, Japanese and Farsi;
Greek, French and Polish;
Thai, Hindi and Swedish –
All woven into the tapestry
Of one country.

Our citizens cover all religions.
America welcomes Catholics to its altars,
As well as Buddhists and Taoists.
We have room for Muslims and Jews,
Methodists and Presbyterians,
Scientologists and Quakers,
Amish and Baptists,
We welcome the Greek Orthodox and the Mystic.
Our sun shines on Christian and Pagan alike.
What we have in common is a country.

As individuals, we have various
Points of view.
That is our strength. Our many cultures,
Races, religions and beliefs, come together
To look through different eyes at the
Same problems.
Because we are linked together
By a flag, by a government,
By a Constitution,
We can interlace our answers together.

QUANDARY

We meet.
The gently blowing wind
Disturbs the light green leaves of spring
A supposed beginning.

The wind blows more away
Than what it keeps.
It throws sound to places far away
Like a ball of music in gloved hands.

And voices speak.
They speak but lose their words
In the currents of air floating by.
What did the voices say?

We meet.
Then we are scattered
Like a thousand petals falling,
A beginning that becomes an end.

MIND GAME

Denny and Matt took turns knocking out the enemy
With their lasers. Gaining points and energy,
They took all night to work to the next level.

Sergeant Dennison Smith reporting for duty, sir.
I have a real weapon now and am ready to
Confront the enemy.

Private Matthew Powers reporting for duty, sir.
I'm good with a joystick, better with an attack rifle,
I learned in my living room.

Denny scored points as the game displayed the man
In combat fatigues and a backpack filled with gear.
He was after a character of a race other than his own.

Matt watched his friend. Challenged by Denny's score,
He decided to show what he was made of.
He grabbed the gun handle and shot the man running.

Dennison saw the men dressed like the characters
In the video game – long white robes and long beards
Just like scoring back home.

Matthew noticed them too. Stationed not far
From his friend, the men in Salwar Kameez
Moved together, like Middle Eastern game pieces.

It was time to shut down for the night. Each boy saved
His score to bring the game back up again.
Imaginary men lived to fight another day.

Dennison and Matthew fired. The men fell to the ground.
Unlike the game, they were gone forever.
They approached the bodies to add up their points.

ONE BLUE STAR

(A Sonnet)

When Alexander's legions proved their strength,
Heroic merit won, his swift reward
Was One Blue Star provided them, for length
Of servitude, for heroes in his guard.

The Blue Star came to Washington's attention.
Two men who were exceptionally brave,
Fought with the best and highest of intentions,
Earned blue star medals for the help they gave.

Then Army Captain Queissner did design
A Blue Star banner, in honor of his sons,
Embattled on the enemy's front line,
The banner hung till days of service done.

Now in my window hangs that same blue star,
Until you come back to me from afar.

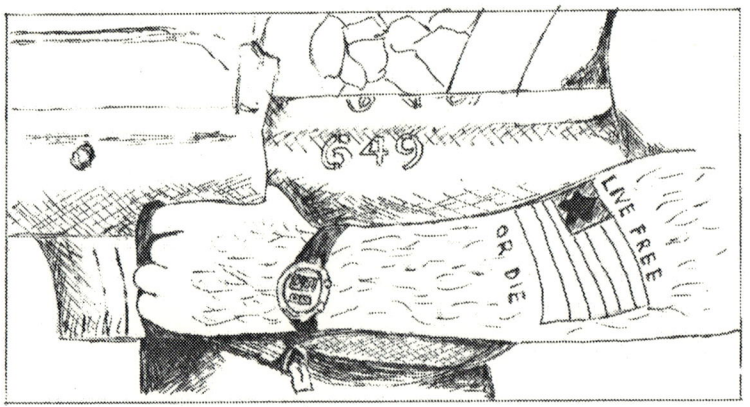

SUNSHINE PATRIOT

The car sat at the light,
Plastic handles supporting flags
From its back windows.
A faded bumper sticker proclaimed
"These colors don't run."
The sun illuminated a tattoo
On the driver's arm
Another flag.

In the next lane, a car idled.
Its plain, white body
Sported no flags fluttering.
No stickers speaking words
Of defiance – only one that said,
"Let there be peace."
The woman waited until the light changed.
And glanced at the sunshine patriot.

She saw his sneer.
They did not agree.
There was no way for
Him to know she wore her flag
internally.
She smiled at him and thought of her son
Serving in a war she didn't understand.

EMBRYO

Three AM.
I lie catatonic in a bed
With graphic flowers on the coverlet,
Brain spinning like a squeaky wheel.

The television's on.
Infrared cameras record
Proof of collateral damage.
Howitzers fire incendiaries into villages.

Unnerved,
I take a glass and pour
Another drink to ease my fears,
To calm my mind's revulsion to death.

Out again,
Into the light of day and beyond
I stagger, trying to reason why
Man solves problems this way.

I work.
I gather the nerve to smile.
And see each person as unique.
People around me talk of dying.

Dying.
I think of that word now,
As I pull the graphic flowers
Over my head and try to rest.

I burrow
Deep in the covers while soldiers
Fight on foreign soil
And plant themselves in their own gardens.

THE MILL

Everyday,
Turning, turning.
The mill wheel grinds.
Instead of water,
Or meal or grain,
This mill turns over
Words and phrases.
Like propaganda in
Animal Farm.

Words are changed,
Ground to the point
That they are pointless.
War is peace
Peace is war.
Words become
Weapons of
Mass destruction.

CONSTITUTION BLUES

"The glue that holds this country together – that keeps us working together, pulling together and respecting each other – is the Constitution."~anon

Have you read it?
Have you experienced it?
Do you know about it?
Is it something someone else
Mentioned to you?

Do you know what it says
About guns,
About marriage,
About abortion?
Does it say anything?

If we change it,
Tailor it to our
Present condition,
Aren't we tinkering
With our foundation?

It has made us
Unique among nations.
Yet we want to micro engineer
Those words, use them
Against one another.

"We hold these truths,"
Or so it says,
We rewrite those truths
To say what we
Want them to say.

When we dabble with the notion
Of excluding a group from its
Protection because we disagree,
The Constitution is no longer
Strong.

MEDITATIONS IN AN OLIVE GROVE

I placed my mat under the branches
Of an olive tree. It was summer
And the sun cast shadows on the ground.
The birds moved like dancers over the grass
Seeking an audience.

The breeze moved the leaves slightly,
Making them sound like muffled wind chimes.
Here in the ripeness of the day,
I thought about the shadows in my soul,
Seeking peace.

How could this day be real?
How could my breath be still enough
To perform my meditation?
I sat, Buddha like, trying to gain control
Of my mind.

I closed my eyes. The movie playing on
My retina took my breath away.
War was there. The ugly, brutal
Destruction of life. I opened my eyes to see
Squirrels running.

A young boy played nearby. He tossed a
Plane into the air and watched it fall.
I saw his face, his shape, his youth,
And prayed he'd never know the sounds
Of war.

FIRST BATTLE

He slept on top of a Bradley
Fighting Vehicle. Two days across the border
And nothing to shoot at.
"Bring it on," said this man,
A combination of Duke and
Schwartzenegger, ready for battle.

He remembered Basic Training,
All the drills and marches with
Full gear, target practice
With the shapes of men to
Shoot at. No different from
Nintendo. Just score a hit.

It was time. The call went out
To attack the position. With confidence,
He unshouldered his weapon,
Ready to go in. He rounded the corner,
Into the fire, men running for cover.
This was no game.

Through the smoke and confusion
He saw a steel object pointing his
Direction. He reacted instinctively
With the ack ack of bullets.
He looked around and ran for cover,
Protecting himself.

After it was over, after the enemy
Disbanded, he walked to the place
Where he'd seen the steel shining.
There, he found the remains of a soldier,
A boy mostly, blood around him,
Body lying at a strange angle.

He recoiled, not outside where people
Would notice, but inside himself,
When he knew he had taken his first life.
The targets in training were effigies
Of men, now real, slaughtered
For a cause.

CONVINCERS

We fight for freedom, so they say.
No one is there to take it from us
But ourselves.

We fight for justice, so we hear.
Justice for the strong.
The weak fall far behind.

We fight to sustain our beliefs.
What if others differ?
Do they not believe as well?

We are barraged by words and images.
Convincing us to think in a straight line,
When the world is curved.

VETERAN'S DAY

He remembered Tommy Reid, a strong young man from Iowa
    With bold muscles from working on his father's farm.
    He'd enlisted when he was 17, lying to the recruiter.
    If he could get to the European theater
    He could take on Hitler singlehandedly.

He remembered Jack Dunnegin, A cousin on his father's side,
    Sometimes in trouble, sometimes a loner,
    Who saw his number in the draft and enlisted the next day,
    He comforted his mother, telling her he would be back
    As soon as his country allowed him to return.

He recalled a man named Cleveland Jakes whose dark skin
    Gleamed on the field of battle. Proud of his heritage,
    He fought with bravery against a stronger foe.
    He battled poverty, racism, misunderstanding,
    But evened the odds in a rice paddy far away.

He'd heard stories about Kate Henson, an Army nurse
    Who fought to keep men alive. She sewed them up
    With threads of her own hair when the sutures were gone.
    She cradled them in her arms as they took their last breath.
    She died inside every time she dressed one more corpse.

He remembered those who fought for liberty, honor, dignity.
    They were patriotic, brave; they did not dishonor themselves in
    Battle. He rolled his wheelchair to the window to watch the
    Flag raising. He thought of his patriotic friends
    Who were all dead.

WORTH FIGHTING FOR

Put your gun aside, soldier, and join the fight,
There are battles to be won with a pen, not a sword;
With a mind, not brute strength;
With diplomacy, not force.

A child is hungry in Arkansas.
She wails as her mother tries to make her understand
The food is gone. There's no job and money's slim.
It's hard to work with childcare so expensive.

Pass them a lifeline, soldier.
Shoot out the stench of poverty with the
Weapon of social action.

A man is ill in Kansas,
He's old and has some money saved
To pass on to his children. But nursing care
Takes every penny, until he's poor enough for aide.

Why are we wealthy, soldiers,
But can't take care of our families? Why must the old ones
Decide between bread and medications?

A man in Michigan can't read.
He grew up with non reading parents who grew up the same.
Words mean nothing to him, he can't find work
In the factories, until he can read instructions.

Draw a line in the sand of illiteracy.
Soldier, pick up the weapon of words
And break the cycle.

A black man cries out in Tennessee,
He is intelligent and gifted but can't climb past the barriers.
Barriers set by others who don't allow him to advance.
He is passed over time and time again.

Oh, soldier, can't you see injustice being done?
Is it not patriotic to give to your country by laying down your gun
To attack the things worth fighting for?

THE RETURN

The letter finally came
Stating a month, a day, an hour.
Written with the Army seal.
Official.
He'd been gone so long,
Could this really be the moment?

She grabbed her calendar,
Circling the date in red,
Elated but fearful,
What if this was a false alarm,
And he was delayed again?

But the day came, cold, rainy,
No symbol of joy, except for that
One sweet circle on the fifth of
February. She dressed like she was
Going to an interview.

She smoothed her hair,
And her daughter's, too, saying,
"Your daddy's coming home today,"
Almost afraid to tell her in case
It was a mirage.

She parked her car, grabbed the
Small, soft hand of the little girl,
And rode the shuttle bus the
Rest of the way,
Other people everywhere.

They stayed in the armory
Protected from the rain,
Planes later than expected.
What if they crashed now in front of
All these people? What if?

The loudspeaker said, "They're here,"
And she, her daughter and all the others
Stood with their umbrellas in the rain,
On a cold February morning,
Watching the lights appear in the sky.

One by one the planes touched down,
The rain stopped for a while, an omen?
Rows of soldiers deplaned in
Neat single rows,
Where was he?

She held their daughter in her arms
As soldiers walked by in
Single file. She craned her neck,
Looking for the one among
The many.

The crowd applauded, called our cheers,
As one soldier passed by
Crippled from battle, yet walking,
Determined to join in the parade.
Someone was lucky, she thought.

The last row came by without her soldier.
The rain began again.
Perplexed, she took her daughter
Back into the armory to be
With the others.

As she entered, she saw the troops
In formation. Hundreds of them in neat lines.
Third row, fifth soldier, standing straight and tall,
She saw him. His eye caught hers.
A small smile broke his steel Army gaze.

Her tears came without warning.
She held their daughter higher,
And pointed him out,
"There's your daddy," she said.
The little girl squealed.

When the soldiers broke ranks,
The tall man came to her,
They held one another without
Speaking, too much to say,
She thanked God for her gift.

Some families are left alone,
War is like that.
But the prayer always is,
And always will be,
Please, God, let them all return.

ONE BLUE STAR: A LIST TO PONDER

This country has suffered two devastating attacks: December 7, 1941 and September 11, 2001. The first led to a war against tyranny, the second has led to a war on terrorism.

This war on terrorism is not a war in the traditional sense. It is a war of radical beliefs clashing against one another. Just as all Muslims are not terrorists, all Americans are not hawks. Non hawks love their country just as much, but pray for peaceful solutions to problems.

War is not always avoidable, but it doesn't seem to work well as a means to lasting peace. With every truce, new enemies made from the previous battle begin to plan the next attack.

Consider these numbers:

America's War Numbers	
Military Service During War	42,348,460
Battle Deaths	**650,954**
Other Deaths in Service (In Theater)	13,853
Other Deaths in Service (Non Theater)	229,661
Non mortal Woundings	1,431,290
Living War Veterans	19,421,266*
Living Veterans	25,497,691*

Statistics from Department of Veterans Affairs
(www.va.gov/pressrel/amwars01.htm)

Our soldiers are valuable. They love this country and want to protect it. Why should they be wasted on a battle that is not necessary? They perform to the utmost and give until they are worn out. They get little pay for their efforts and are pulled away from their families for long periods of time, losing their jobs and their innocence. Deployment should be the LAST RESORT to retain the peace of the world. Why should we waste precious blood?

Our battles have cost the lives of enough young men and women to populate the cities of Knoxville, Tennessee or Baltimore, Maryland. Can we afford to lose more of our citizens? If we must fight, let there be a clear and visible reason for the battle. If not, the fray is not worth the blood of our youth.

ONE BLUE STAR – ABOUT THE BANNER

The design of the Blue Star Banner is attributed to World War I Army Captain Robert L. Queissner who designed it to honor his two sons serving on the front line. Families who had a loved one in the Armed Forces placed the flag inside the front window of their home to let others know they had someone in that family in the military. If two members were serving, the flag bore two stars. Flags could carry as many as five stars, as for the five Sullivan brothers who died on the same ship in World War II.

Theodore Roosevelt's family displayed a flag with a gold star superimposed over the blue one in honor of their son who died in combat in 1918.

It is every family's prayer that their star stays blue.

Want more copies of
ONE BLUE STAR?

Just email mplcreative1@aol.com or
fill out the form (or facsimile thereof) and send to:
Mindy Phillips Lawrence
P.O. Box 778
Park Hills, MO 63601

Name	
Address	
City/State/ZIP	
Number of Copies @ $9.95	
Subtotal	
Sales Tax (MO residence only)	
Postage @ $2.00 1st book, $0.40 each additional book	
Total Enclosed	

ABOUT THE AUTHOR

Photo Credit: Joyce Faulkner

At Little Round Top in Gettysburg, PA
During the Battle of Gettysburg Re Enactment

Mindy Phillips Lawrence, assistant editor of Scribe and Quill, (www.scribequill.com), is the mother of an *Operation Iraqi Freedom* Veteran. Throughout the war, she supported the efforts of the troops while questioning why our young men and women were put in harm's way.

Mindy speaks at writing events, publishes book reviews and interviews, and has work printed in several magazines, including Writer's Digest. She is newsletter editor of the Missouri Writers Guild. Currently, she is researching her first novel about Chicago radio in the 1930s and 1940s.

Mindy has many varied interests, including hot air ballooning, walking, cycling and singing. She lives near St. Louis.

mplcreative1@aol.com

Printed in the United States
22253LVS00002B/131